Paper Creations:

MYTHICAL CREATURE ORIGAMI

Duy Nguyen

STERLING

New York / London

www.sterlingpublishing.com

STERLING and the distinctive Sterling logo are registered trademarks
of Sterling Publishing Co., Inc.

2 4 6 8 10 9 7 5 3 1

Published by Sterling Publishing Co., Inc.
387 Park Avenue South, New York, NY 10016

This book is comprised of material from the following Sterling Publishing Co., Inc. titles:
Fantasy Origami © 2001 by Duy Nguyen
Origami Myths & Legends © 2005 by Duy Nguyen

Distributed in Canada by Sterling Publishing
c/o Canadian Manda Group, 165 Dufferin Street
Toronto, Ontario, Canada M6K 3H6
Distributed in the United Kingdom by GMC Distribution Services
Castle Place, 166 High Street, Lewes, East Sussex, England BN7 1XU
Distributed in Australia by Capricorn Link (Australia) Pty. Ltd.
P.O. Box 704, Windsor, NSW 2756, Australia

Origami paper designs from Paper Source, Inc.
Visit www.paper-source.com for similar items.

Design by Beth Nori

Sterling ISBN-13: 978-1-4027-5348-0
ISBN-10: 1-4027-5348-9

For information about custom editions, special sales, premium and
corporate purchases, please contact Sterling Special Sales
Department at 800-805-5489 or specialsales@sterlingpublishing.com.

CONTENTS

BASIC INSTRUCTIONS

PAPER

The best paper to use for origami will be very thin, keep a crease well, and fold flat. It can be plain white paper, solid-color paper, or wrapping paper with a design only on one side. Regular typing paper may be too heavy to allow the many tight folds needed for some figures. Be aware, too, that some kinds of paper may stretch slightly, either in length or in width, and this may cause a problem in paper folding. Packets of paper especially for use in origami are available from craft and hobby shops.

Unless otherwise indicated, the usual paper used in creating these forms is square, 15 by 15 centimeters or approximately 6 by 6 inches. Some forms may call for half a square, i.e., 3 by 6 inches or, cut diagonally, a triangle. A few origami forms require a more rectangular size or a longer piece of paper. For those who are learning and have a problem getting their fingers to work tight folds, larger sizes of paper can be used. Actually, any size paper squares can be used—slightly larger figures are easier to make than overly small ones. The paper provided within this gift set is 6 by 6 inches, easy to work with for origami novices.

GLUE

Use an easy-flowing but not loose paper glue. Use it sparingly; don't soak the paper. A toothpick makes a good applicator. Allow the glued form time to dry. Avoid using stick glue, as the application pressure needed (especially if the stick has become dry) can damage your figure.

TECHNIQUE

Fold with care. Position the paper, especially at corners, precisely and see that edges line up before creasing a fold. Once you are sure of the fold, use a fingernail to make a clean, flat crease. Don't get discouraged with your first efforts. In time, what your mind can create, your fingers can fashion.

SYMBOLS & LINES

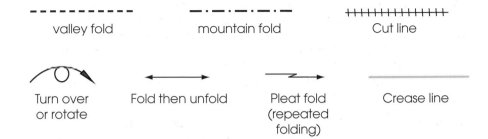

valley fold   mountain fold   Cut line

Turn over
or rotate

Fold then unfold

Pleat fold
(repeated
folding)

Crease line

SQUARING
OFF PAPER

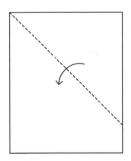

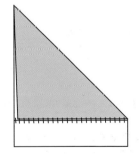

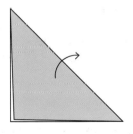

1. Take a rectangular
sheet, and valley
fold diagonally.

2. Cut off excess on
long side as shown.

3. Unfold. Sheet is square.

BASIC FOLDS

KITE FOLD

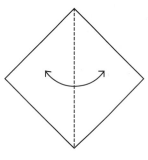

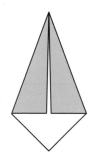

1. Fold and unfold a square diagonally, making a center crease.

2. Fold both sides in to the center crease.

3. This is a kite form.

VALLEY FOLD

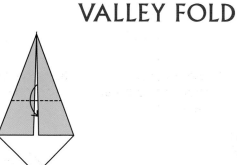

1. Here, using the kite, fold form toward you (forward), making a "valley."

2. This fold forward is a valley fold.

MOUNTAIN FOLD

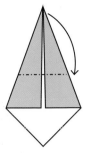

1. Here, using the kite, fold form away from you (backwards), making a "mountain."

2. This fold backwards is a mountain fold.

INSIDE REVERSE FOLD

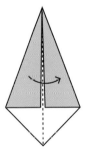

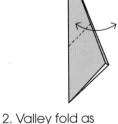

1. Here, using the kite, valley fold closed.

2. Valley fold as marked to crease, then unfold.

3. Pull tip in direction of arrow.

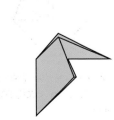

4. Appearance before completion.

5. You've made an inside reverse fold.

OUTSIDE REVERSE FOLD

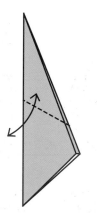

1. Using closed kite, valley fold and unfold.

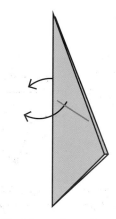

2. Fold inside out, as shown by arrows.

3. Appearance before completion.

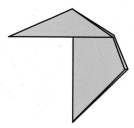

4. You've made an outside reverse fold.

PLEAT FOLD

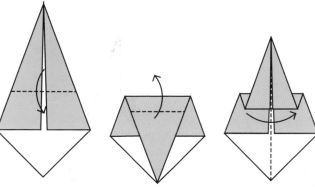
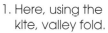

1. Here, using the kite, valley fold.

2. Valley fold back again.

3. This is a pleat. Valley fold in half.

4. You've made a pleat fold.

PLEAT FOLD REVERSE

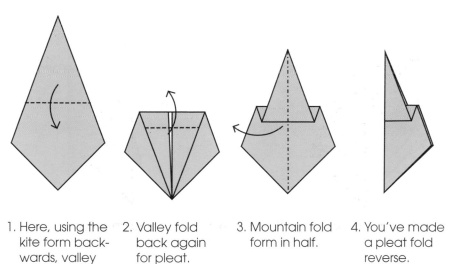

1. Here, using the kite form backwards, valley fold.

2. Valley fold back again for pleat.

3. Mountain fold form in half.

4. You've made a pleat fold reverse.

BASE FOLDS

Base folds are basic forms that do not in themselves produce origami, but serve as a basis, or jumping-off point, for a number of creative origami figures—some quite complex. As when beginning other crafts, learning to fold these base folds is not the most exciting part of origami. They are, however, easy to do, and will help you with your technique. They also quickly become rote, so much so that you can do many using different-colored papers while you are watching television or your mind is elsewhere. With completed base folds handy, if you want to quickly work up a form or are suddenly inspired with an idea for an original, unique figure, you can select an appropriate base fold and swiftly bring a new creation to life.

BASE FOLD I

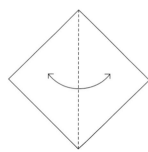

1. Fold and unfold in direction of arrow.

2. Fold both sides in to center crease, then unfold. Rotate.

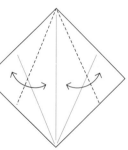

3. Fold both sides in to center crease, then unfold.

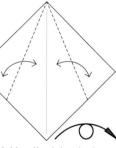

4. Pinch corners of square together and fold inward.

5. Completed Base Fold I.

BASE FOLD II

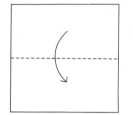

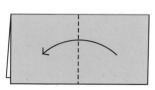

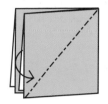

1. Valley fold.

2. Valley fold.

3. Squash fold.

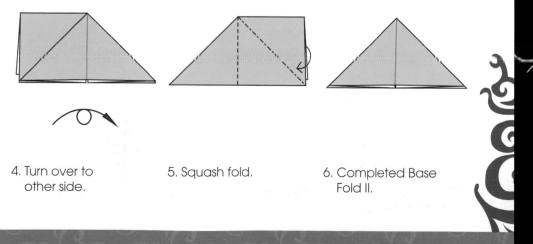

4. Turn over to
   other side.

5. Squash fold.

6. Completed Base
   Fold II.

BASE FOLD III

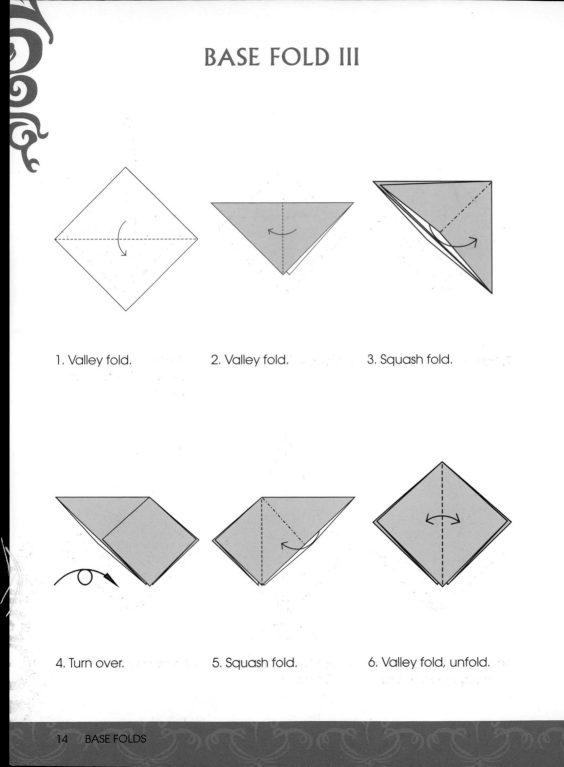

1. Valley fold.

2. Valley fold.

3. Squash fold.

4. Turn over.

5. Squash fold.

6. Valley fold, unfold.

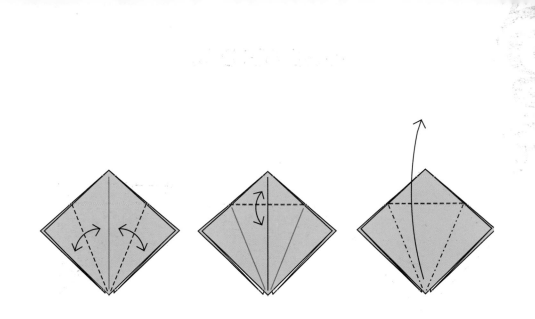

7. Valley folds, unfold.

8. Valley fold, unfold.

9. Pull in direction of arrow, folding inward at sides.

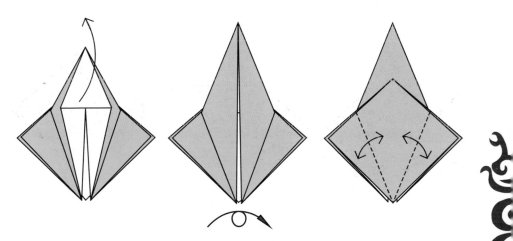

10. Appearance before completion of fold.

11. Fold completed. Turn over.

12. Valley folds, unfold.

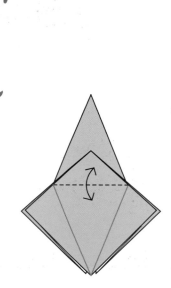

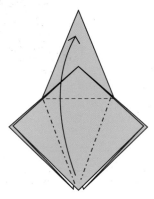

13. Valley fold, unfold.

14. Repeat, again pulling in direction of arrow.

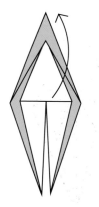

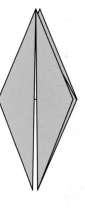

15. Appearance before completion.

16. Completed Base Fold III.

FLYING FOX

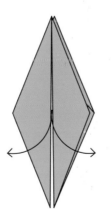

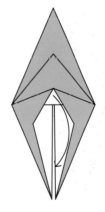

1. Start with Base Fold III; pull open in direction of arrows.

2. Squash fold as shown.

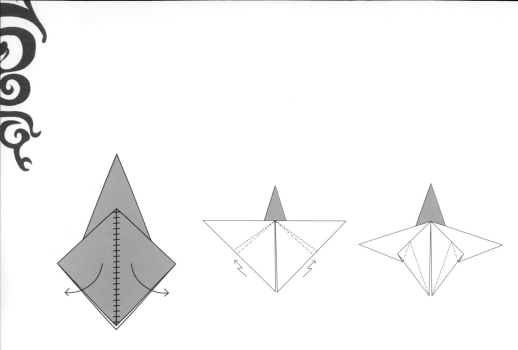

3. Cut, then unfold.

4. Pleat folds on both sides.

5. Squash folds.

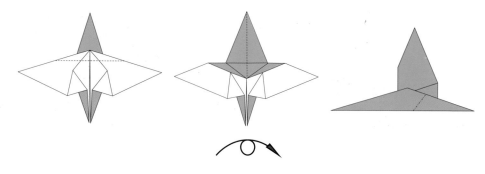

6. Valley fold.

7. Valley fold in half, then rotate form.

8. Inside reverse folds front and back.

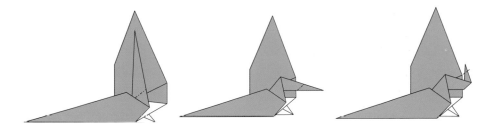

9. Inside reverse folds front and back.

10. Again, Inside reverse folds front and back.

11. Now outside reverse folds front and back.

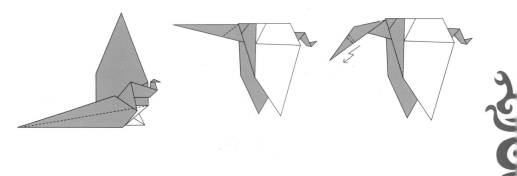

12. Valley folds front and back.

13. Outside reverse fold.

14. Pleat fold.

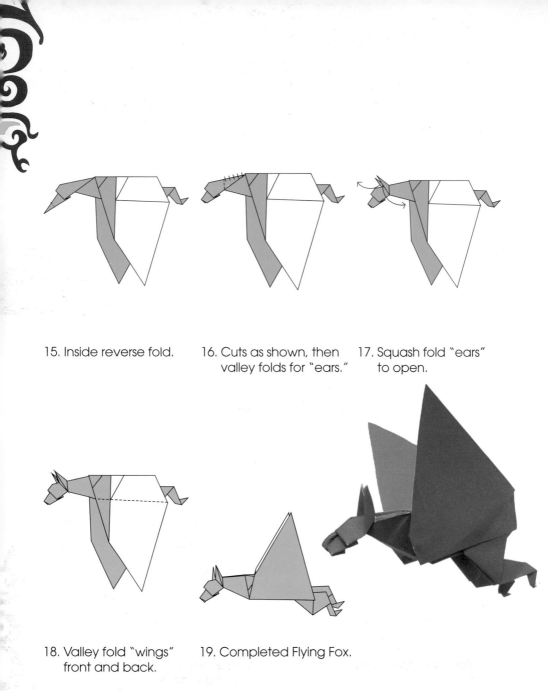

15. Inside reverse fold.

16. Cuts as shown, then valley folds for "ears."

17. Squash fold "ears" to open.

18. Valley fold "wings" front and back.

19. Completed Flying Fox.

WILD DUCK

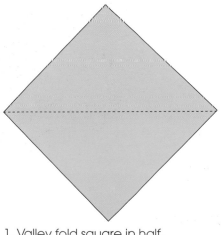

1. Valley fold square in half, diagonally.

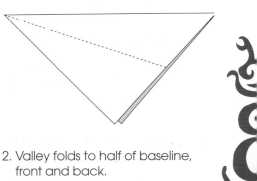

2. Valley folds to half of baseline, front and back.

3. Valley folds front and back, and squash fold as you go.

4. Cuts as shown.

5. Now mountain folds front and back.

6. Inside reverse fold.

7. Another inside reverse fold.

8. Inside reverse fold again.

9. Valley folds, front and back.

10. Mountain fold, to form "tail" end.

11. Outside reverse fold.

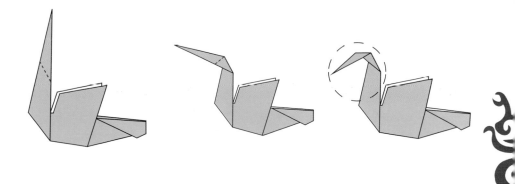

12. Outside reverse fold.

13. Outside reverse fold.

14. Completed fold, see close-ups for head detail.

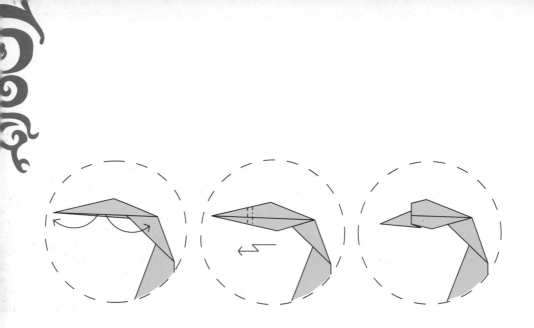

15. Pull to sides and flatten.

16. Pleat fold.

17. Return to full view.

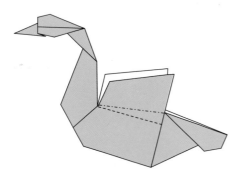

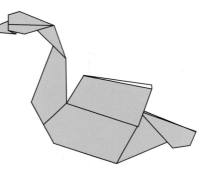

18. Pleat fold "wings" front and back.

19. Completed Wild Duck.

FLYING DRAGON

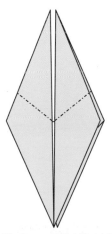

1. Start with Base Fold III. Inside reverse folds.

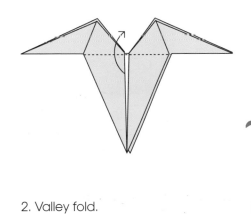

2. Valley fold.

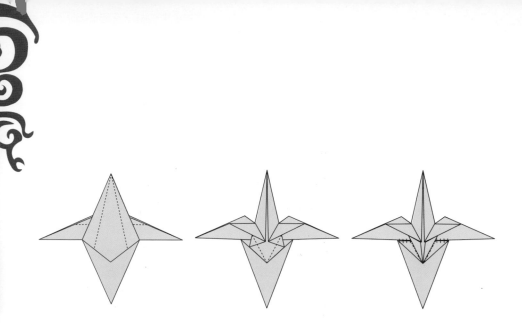

3. Valley folds and squash folds.

4. Valley folds.

5. Make cuts, then mountain folds.

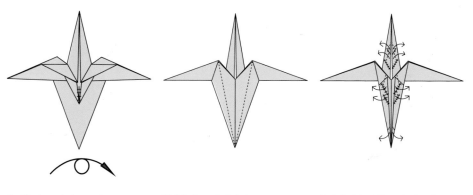

6. Cut point as shown, then turn to other side.

7. Valley folds.

8. Make all cuts to front layer as shown here, then valley fold cut parts.

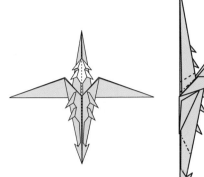

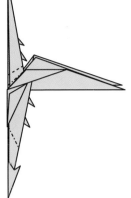

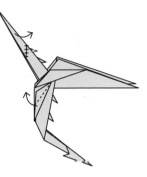

9. Valley fold in half.

10. Crimp fold, and inside reverse fold.

11. Cut and valley unfold. Outside reverse folds front and back.

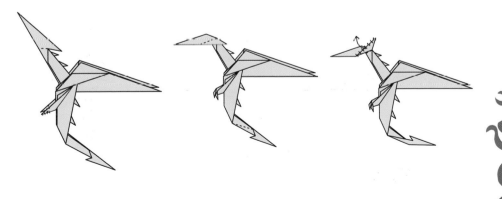

12. Cuts on both folds, then valley folds to sides.

13. Valley folds.

14. Cuts and valley folds front and back.

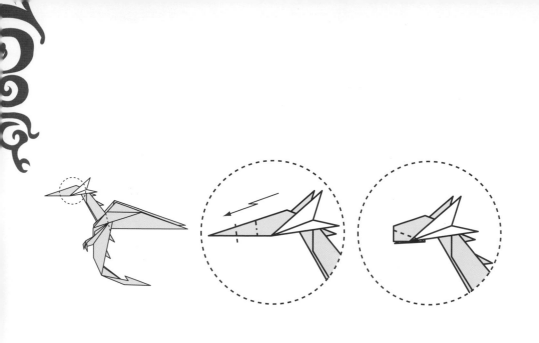

15. Valley folds both
    sides, then see
    close-up views
    for next steps.

16. Pleat fold.

17. Valley fold
    both sides.

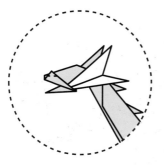

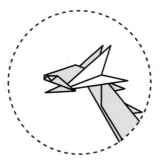

18. Valley fold both sides.

19. Back to full view.

20. Mountain folds both sides.

21. Completed Flying Dragon.

PHOENIX

PART 1

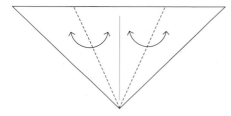
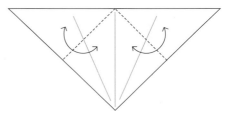

1. Start with a square sheet cut diagonally; valley folds and crease, then unfold.

2. Valley folds again and crease, then unfold.

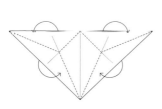

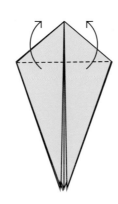

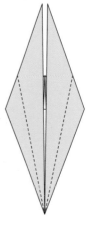

3. Pinch corners together, folding inward along dashed lines.

4. Valley folds.

5. Valley folds.

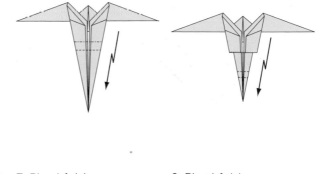

6. Mountain folds.

7. Pleat fold.

8. Pleat fold.

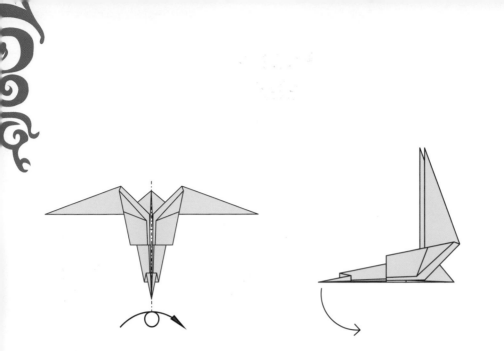

9. Mountain fold in half,
   and rotate form.

10. Pull point downward and crimp
    to position "head."

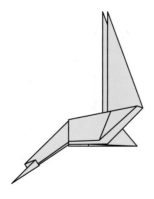

11. Part 1 (front) of phoenix, ready
    for head detail (part 3).

PART 2

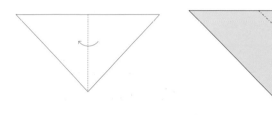

1. Start with a square
   sheet cut diagonally;
   valley fold.

2. Inside reverse fold.

3. Make double cuts for
   width as shown

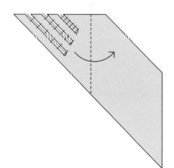

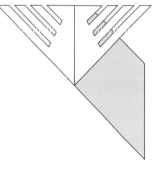

4. Valley fold the first layer.

5. Completed part 2 (back)
   of phoenix.

PART 3

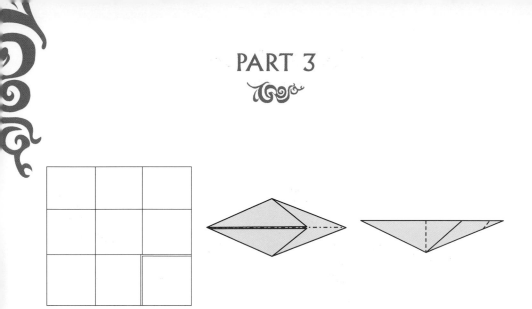

1. Cut 1/9th square of origami paper, and make Base Fold I.

2. Mountain fold in half.

3. Squash fold both sides; outside reverse fold tip.

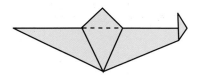

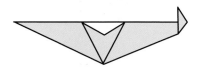

4. Valley fold both sides.

5. Completed part 3 ("head" section) of phoenix.

TO ATTACH

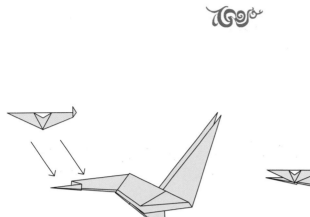

1. Join parts 1 and 3 together; apply glue.

2. Cut off flap as shown.

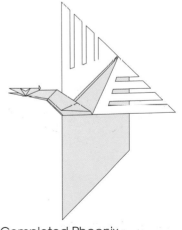

3. Join combined parts 1 and 3 with part 2 as shown, and apply glue to secure.

4. Completed Phoenix.

PEGASUS

PART 1

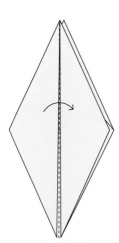

1. Start with Base Fold III and valley
   fold front and back.

2. Cut through layers; valley fold
   front and back again.

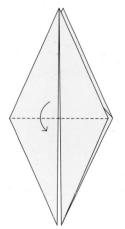

3. Valley fold top layer.

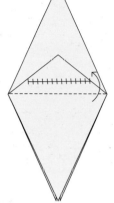

4. Cut off corner, as shown, then valley fold layer back.

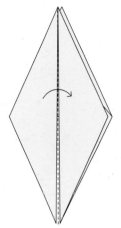

5. Valley fold form in half.

6. Mountain fold front and back layers; inside reverse fold. Rotate.

7. Valley folds front and back.

8. Pleat folds front and back.

9. Pull front "leg" outward and in direction of arrow, squash into position.

10. Outside reverse fold.

11. Valley fold.

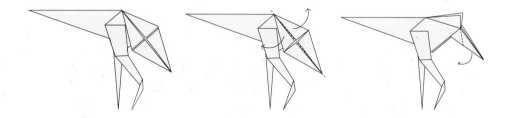

12. Make cuts in layer as indicated.

13. Open cut layers in direction of arrows. Valley fold in half.

14. Valley fold to crease, then outside reverse fold lower layer only.

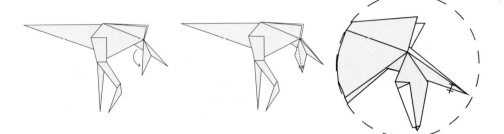

15. Pull paper out from inside of reversed layer and flatten to form "head."

16. Valley fold and cut tip. See close-ups for "head" detail.

17. Cut off other tip.

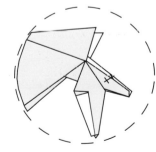

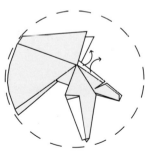

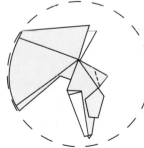

18. Partially cut through both sides as shown.

19. Open upper folds in direction of arrows, and outside reverse fold tip to form "mask."

20. Valley fold both sides.

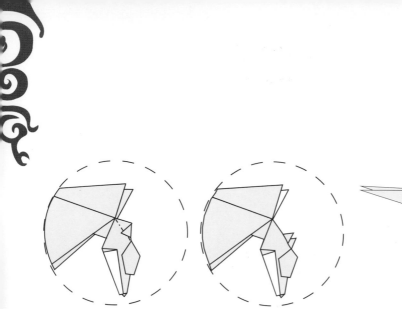

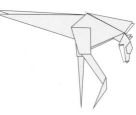

21. Mountain fold both "ears" into head section.

22. Return to full view.

23. Valley fold "mane" to one side.

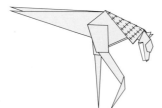

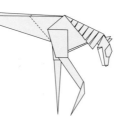

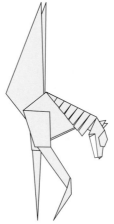

24. Make cuts through layers as indicated.

25. Valley fold "wings" front and back.

26. Completed part 1 (front) of Pegasus.

PART 2

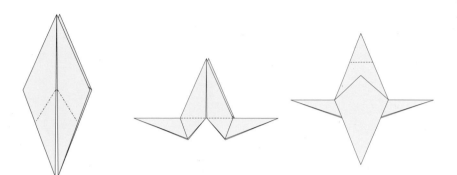

1. Start with Base Fold III, then inside reverse folds.

2. Valley folds.

3. Valley fold.

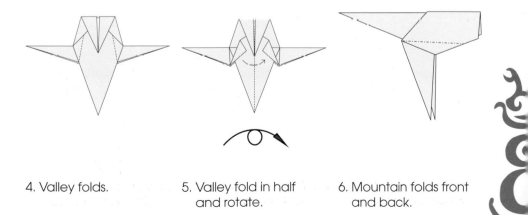

4. Valley folds.

5. Valley fold in half and rotate.

6. Mountain folds front and back.

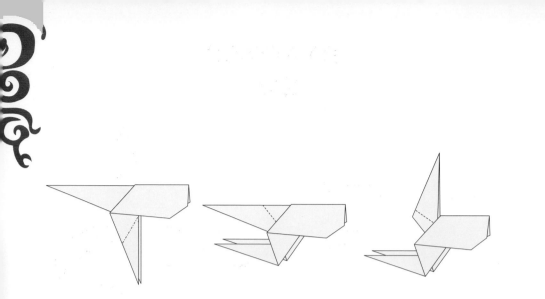

7. Inside reverse folds
   front and back.

8. Outside reverse fold.

9. Outside reverse fold.

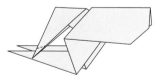

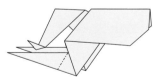

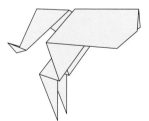

10. Outside reverse fold
    to finish "tail."

11. Inside reverse folds
    front and back.

12. Completed part 2
    (rear) of Pegasus.

TO ATTACH

1. Attach parts 1 and 2 of Pegasus, and glue to hold.

2. Completed Pegasus.

UNICORN

PART 1

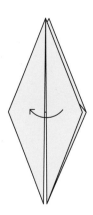

1. Start with Base Fold III. Valley fold in half.

2. Valley fold. Repeat behind.

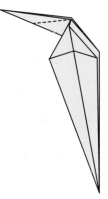

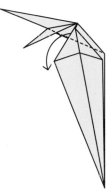

3. Inside reverse fold.

4. Outside reverse fold outside layer only.

5. Valley fold.

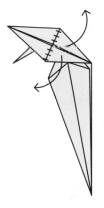

6. Cuts and valley unfolds.

7. Valley fold.

8. Unfolds and valley fold.

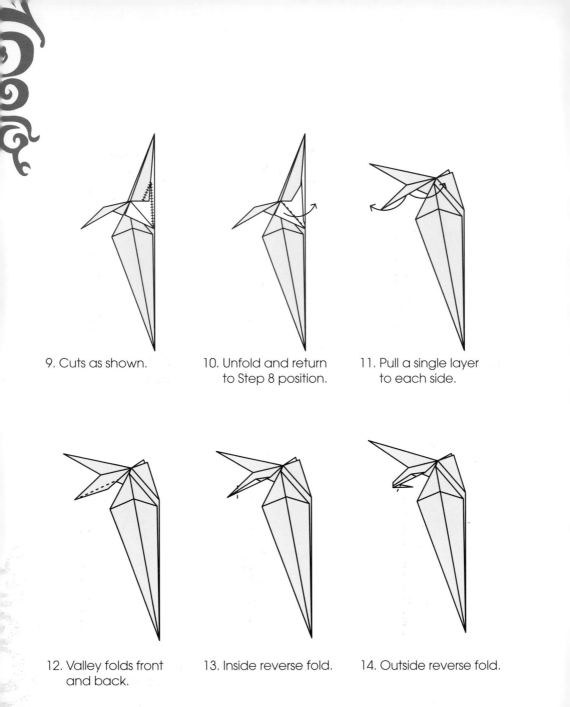

9. Cuts as shown.

10. Unfold and return to Step 8 position.

11. Pull a single layer to each side.

12. Valley folds front and back.

13. Inside reverse fold.

14. Outside reverse fold.

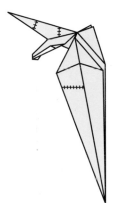

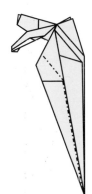

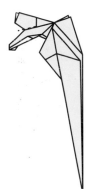

15. Cuts as shown.

16. Mountain folds.

17. Outside reverse folds.

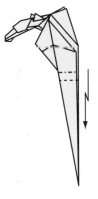

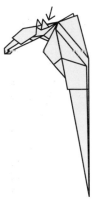

18. Pleat folds.

19. Pleat fold.

20. Tuck both side flaps inside.

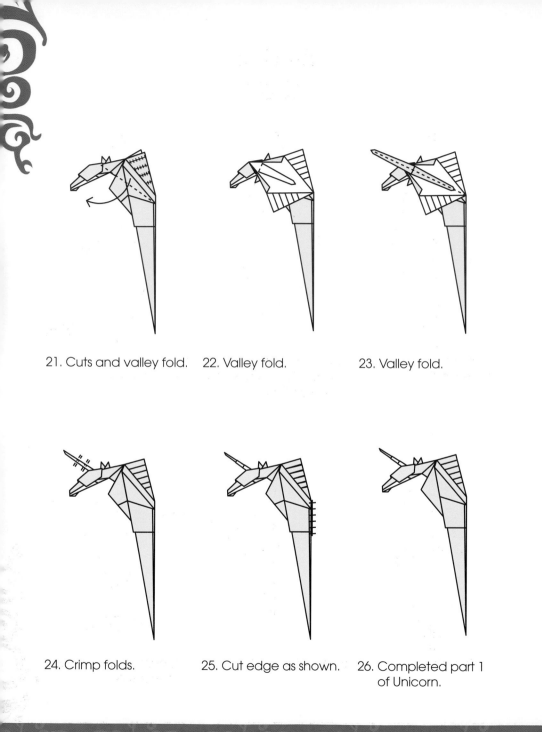

21. Cuts and valley fold.   22. Valley fold.   23. Valley fold.

24. Crimp folds.   25. Cut edge as shown.   26. Completed part 1
                                                     of Unicorn.

PART 2

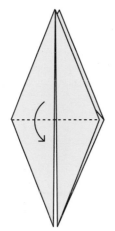

1. Start with Base Fold III.
   Valley fold.

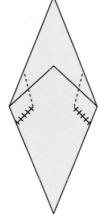

2. Cuts as shown
   through all layers and
   valley folds.

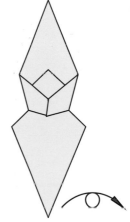

3. Turn over
   to other side.

4. Valley folds.

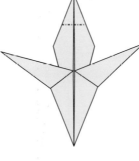

5. Mountain fold.

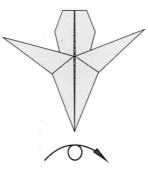

6. Mountain fold in half,
   then rotate.

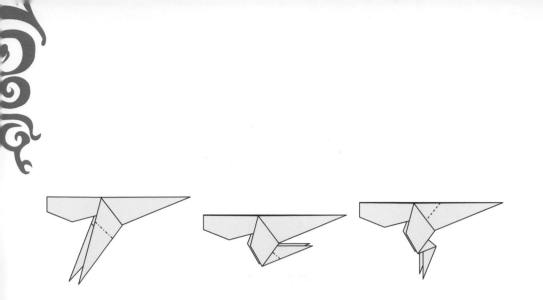

7. Inside reverse folds
front and back.

8. Inside reverse folds
front and back.

9. Inside reverse fold.

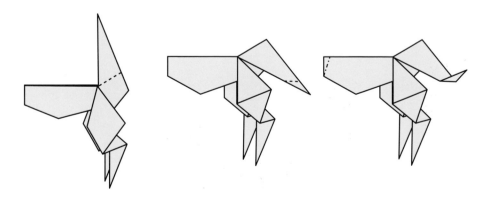

10. Inside reverse fold.

11. Outside reverse fold.

12. Inside reverse fold.

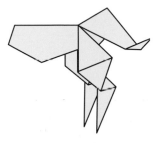

13. Completed part 2 of Unicorn.

TO ATTACH

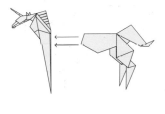

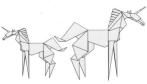

1. Join both parts together. Apply glue to hold and separate legs for standing.

2. Completed Unicorn.

SPHINX

PART I

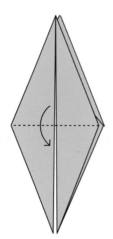

1. Start with Base Fold III.
   Valley fold.

2. Cut as shown.

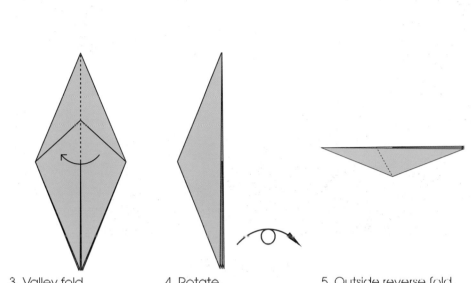

3. Valley fold.

4. Rotate.

5. Outside reverse fold.

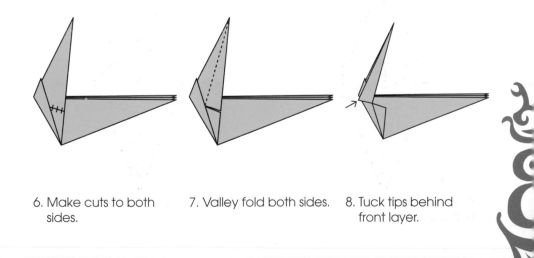

6. Make cuts to both
   sides.

7. Valley fold both sides.

8. Tuck tips behind
   front layer.

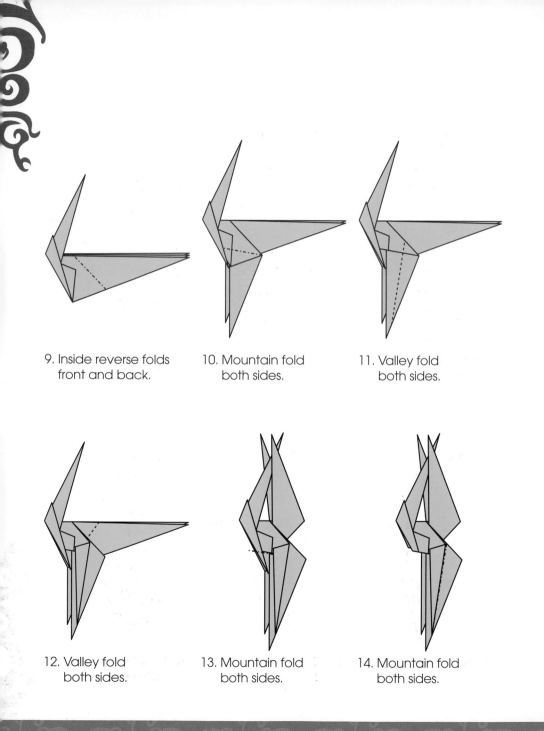

9. Inside reverse folds
front and back.

10. Mountain fold
both sides.

11. Valley fold
both sides.

12. Valley fold
both sides.

13. Mountain fold
both sides.

14. Mountain fold
both sides.

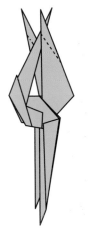

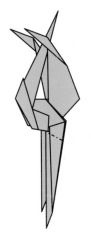

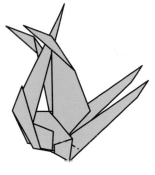

15. Valley fold both sides.

16. Inside reverse folds both sides.

17. Inside reverse folds both sides.

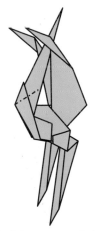

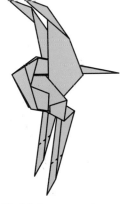

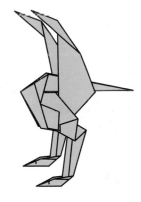

18. Inside reverse fold.

19. Outside reverse folds.

20. Outside reverse folds both feet.

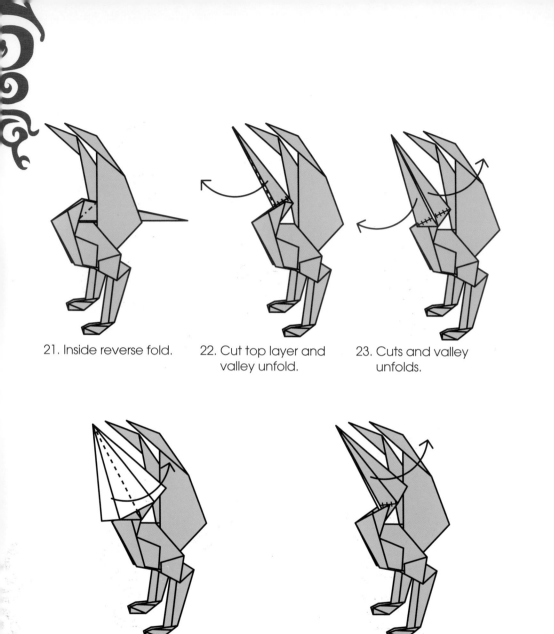

21. Inside reverse fold.

22. Cut top layer and valley unfold.

23. Cuts and valley unfolds.

24. Valley fold.

25. Cut and valley folds.

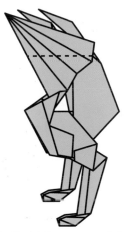

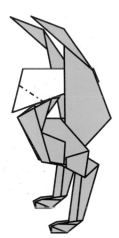

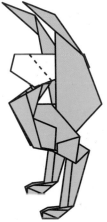

26. Outside reverse fold. 27. Inside reverse fold. 28. Valley fold both
                                                          sides.

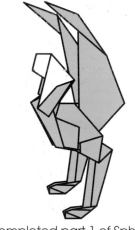

29. Completed part 1 of Sphinx.   30. Or, with wings forward.

PART 2

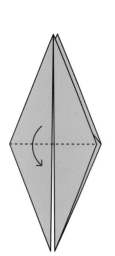

1. Start with Base Fold III
   and valley fold.

2. Turn over to the
   other side.

3. Make cuts and
   mountain folds.

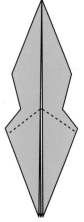

4. Valley folds.

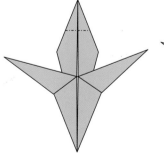

5. Mountain fold.

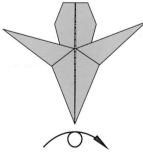

6. Mountain fold in
   half and rotate.

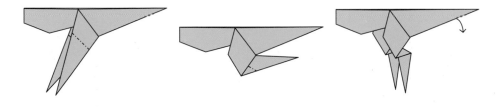

7. Inside reverse fold
   front and back.

8. Inside reverse folds
   both sides.

9. Pull and crimp into
   position.

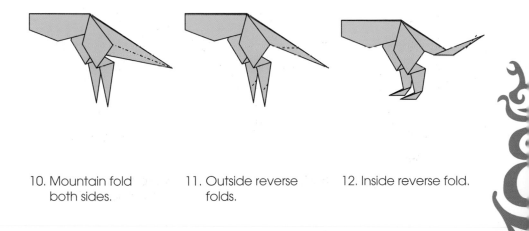

10. Mountain fold
    both sides.

11. Outside reverse
    folds.

12. Inside reverse fold.

13. Valley unfolds.

14. Outside reverse folds both feet.

15. Completed part 2 of Sphinx.

TO ATTACH

1. Join both parts together as shown and apply glue to hold.

2. Completed Sphinx.

CENTAUR

PART 1

1. Start with Base Fold III.
   Inside reverse folds.

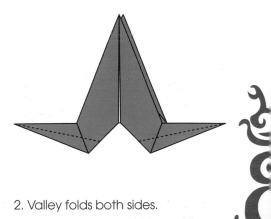

2. Valley folds both sides.

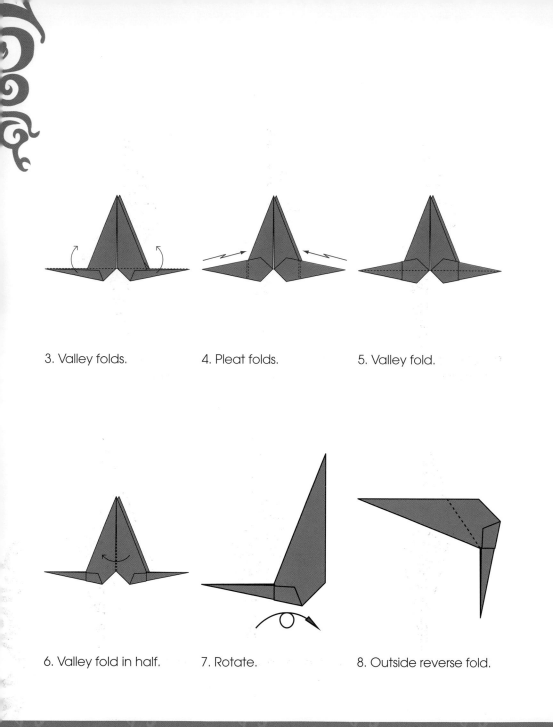

3. Valley folds.

4. Pleat folds.

5. Valley fold.

6. Valley fold in half.

7. Rotate.

8. Outside reverse fold.

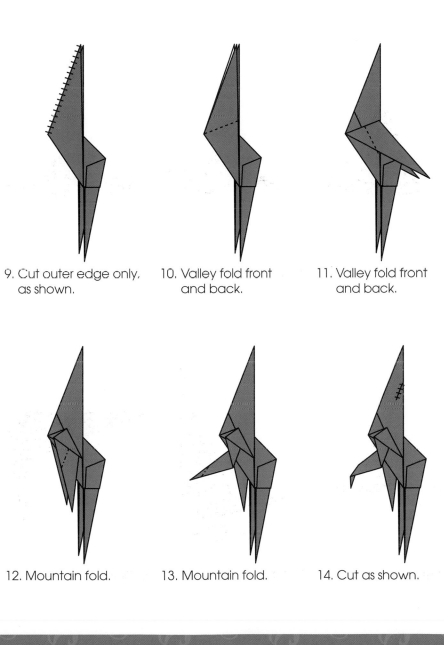

9. Cut outer edge only, as shown.

10. Valley fold front and back.

11. Valley fold front and back.

12. Mountain fold.

13. Mountain fold.

14. Cut as shown.

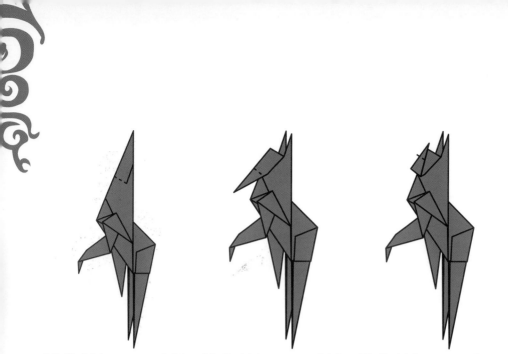

15. Outside reverse fold.

16. Outside reverse fold.

17. Outside reverse fold.

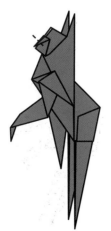

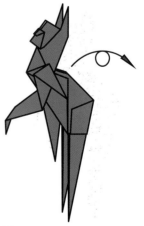

18. Inside reverse fold.

19. Cut and mountain fold. Repeat behind.

20. Turn over to other side.

21. Mountain fold.

22. Mountain fold.

23. Mountain fold.

24. Valley fold.

25. Pull and squash fold.

26. Completed part 1 of Centaur.

PART 2

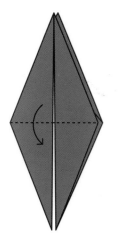

1. Start with Base Fold III. Valley fold.

2. Turn over to other side.

3. Cuts and mountain folds.

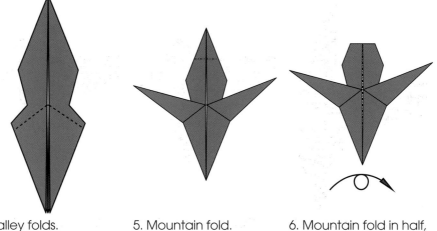

4. Valley folds.

5. Mountain fold.

6. Mountain fold in half, then rotate.

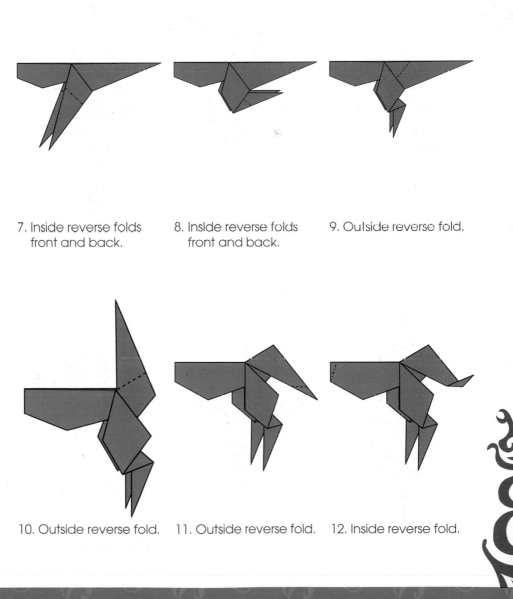

7. Inside reverse folds front and back.

8. Inside reverse folds front and back.

9. Outside reverse fold.

10. Outside reverse fold.

11. Outside reverse fold.

12. Inside reverse fold.

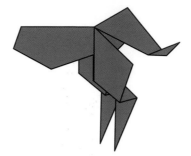

13. Complete part 2 of Centaur.

PART 3

1. Valley fold 2″ by 5″ (5 by 13 cm) sheet.

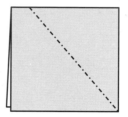

2. Inside reverse fold.

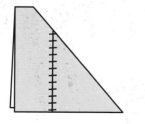

3. Cut as shown.

4. Cuts and mountain fold front and back.

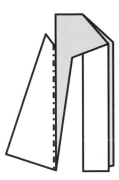
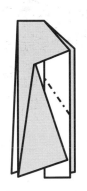

5. Mountain folds front and back.

6. Inside reverse fold.

7. Complete part 3 of Centaur.

TO ATTACH

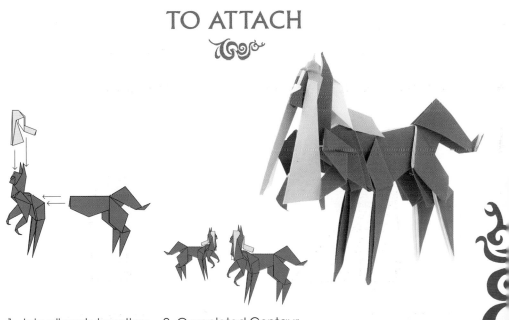

1. Join all parts together as shown. Apply glue to hold.

2. Completed Centaur.

HYDRA

PART 1

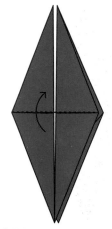

1. Start with Base Fold III. Cut front layer only, as shown.

2. Valley fold.

3. Inside reverse folds.

4. Cut as shown, then valley fold.

5. Cut and valley fold.

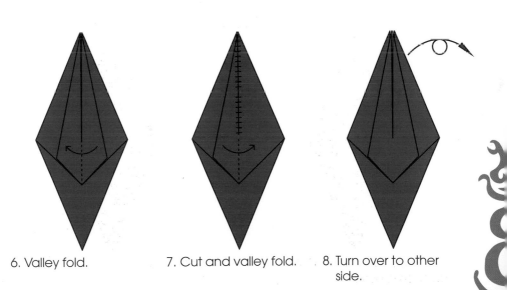

6. Valley fold.

7. Cut and valley fold.

8. Turn over to other side.

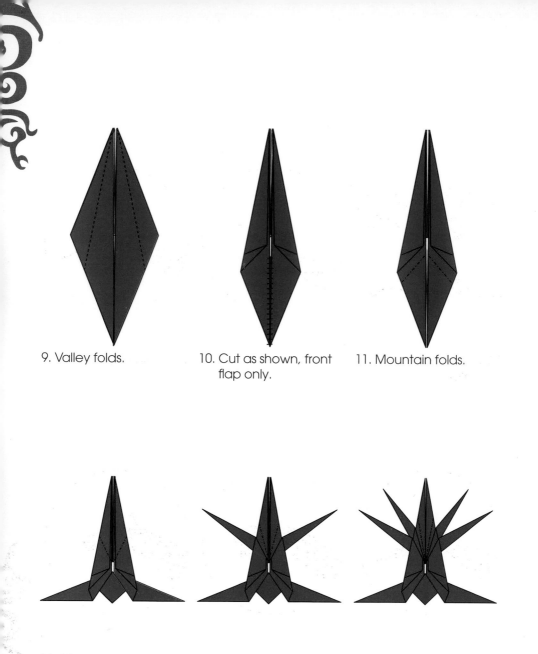

9. Valley folds.

10. Cut as shown, front flap only.

11. Mountain folds.

12. Mountain folds.

13. Mountain folds.

14. Mountain folds.

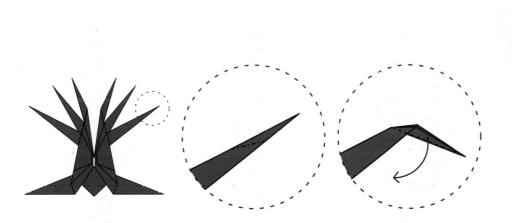

15. See close-ups for detail.

16. Inside reverse fold.

17. Valley fold.

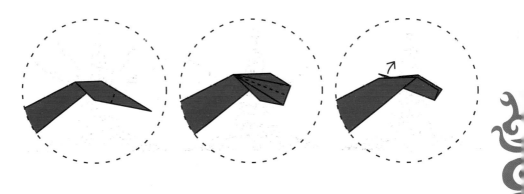

18. Valley fold.

19. Valley fold.

20. Pull and squash fold into place.

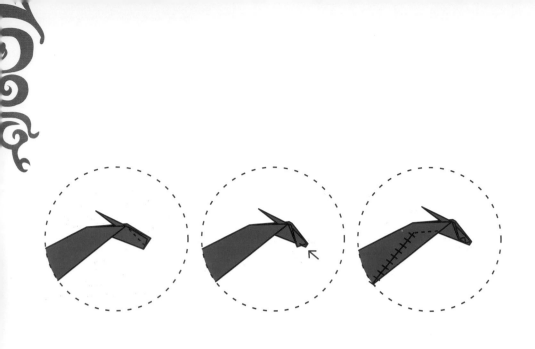

21. Valley fold both sides.

22. Valley fold both sides.

23. Cut as shown and valley fold to sides.

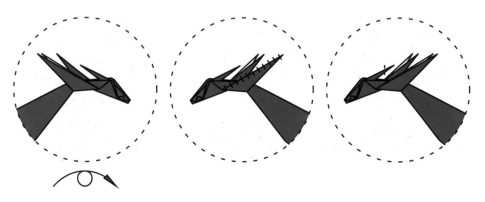

24. Turn over to other side.

25. Cut edge as shown.

26. Inside reverse fold.

27. Valley folds out to sides. Turn over.

28. Return to full view.

29. For other "heads," repeat Steps 16 through 28. Valley folds.

30. Outside reverse folds.

31. Outside reverse folds.

32. Outside reverse folds.

33. Inside reverse folds.

34. Mountain fold in half.

35. Completed part 1 of Hydra.

PART 2

1. Start with Base Fold III. Cuts to top layer.

2. Valley fold.

3. Inside reverse folds.

4. Cut, then turn over to other side.

5. Valley fold both sides.

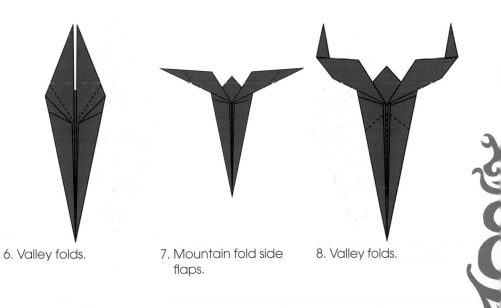

6. Valley folds.

7. Mountain fold side flaps.

8. Valley folds.

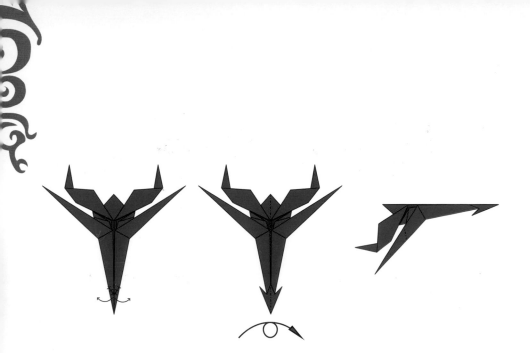

9. Cuts. Valley open to sides.

10. Mountain fold in half, then rotate.

11. Inside reverse folds.

12. Inside reverse folds.

13. Rotate.

14. Pleat folds.

15. Pull and squash into place to add curve.

16. Completed part 2 of Hydra.

TO ATTACH

1. Join both parts together and apply glue to hold. Position heads, and open out figure to stand.

2. Completed Hydra.

INDEX